PAN AMERICAN FLIGHT #863
to Paradise!

*From the author's small town of Panganiban to the vast plains of America,
including collection of inspirational poems & other literary works.*
(Sequel to the "The Thing of Beauty is a Joy Forever")

VOLUME III

FRANK A. DE LA ROSA

Copyright © Frank A. De La Rosa. All rights reserved.

No part of this publication may be reproduced, distributed, or transmitted in any form or by any means, including photocopying, recording, or other electronic or mechanical methods, without the prior written permission of the publisher, except in the case of brief quotations embodied in reviews and certain other non-commercial uses permitted by copyright law.

ISBN: 978-1-958895-38-2 (Hardcover Edition)
ISBN: 978-1-958895-39-9 (E-book Edition)

Printed in the United States.

CONTENTS

Section   *Pages*

Slow Me Down, Lord	9
Footprints In The Sand	15
Looking Back...There Are So Much To Be Thankful For	18
Panaguican Hill	24
Office Of The Municipal Mayor Message	27
The Discovery Of Murphy's Law	30
Personal Story	36
There Is No Distance In Prayer	36
Food For Thought	39
People Who Know How To Brighten A Day	42
May You Always Have An Angel By Your Side	45
Day To Day Life Vs. Christian Life	48
Things To Remember When Your Parents Got Old:	51
Souls....	57
God Knows No Stranger	59
Inspirational Quotations:	62
Persistence	65
Living Life One Day At A Time	68
Inspirational Thoughts To Ponder:	71
The Visitor	74
Inspirational Thoughts To Ponder:	77
Don't We All?	80
Knights Helping Knight	82
The Gift Of Faith	85
To: Ms. Novett P. Mckenzie	91

Let's Be A Team 94
Portrait Of Friendship 97
Thank You Lord. 100
Just For Laughs 103
The Beautiful Act Of Giving 106
The Rose Within 109
Photography. 111
Live A Life That Matters 112
Food For Thought 115
Ox Tail Kare-Kare 116
Our Deepest Fear... 117
Dear Lord 119
Live Up To Your Dreams! 120
Letter From Heaven 122
One Solitary Man 123
Oblations (From "Do It Anyway" -Version 125
By Mother Teresa Of Calcutta) 125
I Have Never Moved A Mountain 126
The Serenity Prayer 128
The American National Anthem 129

SLOW ME DOWN, LORD

Slow me down, lord.
Ease the pounding of my heart by the quieting of my mind.
Steady my hurried pace.
Give me, amidst the day's confusion,
the calmness of the everlasting hills.

Break the tension of my nerves and muscles
with the soothing music of singing stream
that live in my memory.

Help me to know the magical, restoring of sleep.
Teach me the art
of taking minute vacations...
slowing down to look at a flower.
to chat with a friend.
to read a few lines from a good book.

Remind me
of the fable of the hare and the tortoise,
that the race is not always the swift,
that there is more to life than measuring its speed.

let me look at the branches of the towering oak
and know that...it grew slowly...and well.

Inspire me to send my own roots down deep...
to the soil of life's enduring values.

That I may grow toward the stars of my greater destiny.
SLOW ME DOWN, LORD.

This book is lovingly dedicated to
my youngest son, Francis,
PE with his wife, Quyen, MD (OB-GYN)
with their 3 children Aileen, Leiya and Anderson.

Frank A. De La Rosa, the father of Francis.

Mary Grace De La Rosa, the mother of Francis

Ready to bloom Magnolia in my garden.

Snakes don't like this plant. TANGLAD. Surround your garden with Lemon Grass to drive snakes away. From experience!

I found this beautiful Amaryllis flower blooming in my yard after 5 years & forgotten. A gift from Joy Cruz.

We cannot blame time for our frailties and physical changes, as we go along our life's journey. Let's just face it whatever comes along. Life is a journey, and not a destination. Life on earth is just a passing scene. Let's enjoy every second of it.

FOOTPRINTS IN THE SAND

One night I dreamed I was walking along the beach with the Lord
Scenes from my life flashed across the sky,
In each, I noticed footprints in the sand.
Sometimes there were two sets of footprints;
other times there was only one.

During the lowest times of my life
I could see only one set of footprints,
so I said, "Lord, you promised me,
that you would walk with me always.
Why, when I have needed you most would you leave me?"

The Lord replied, "My precious child,
I love you and would never leave you.
The times when you have seen only one set of footprints,
it was then that I carried you."

A Family Get-Together at the Young's Buffet Chinese Restaurant in Palm Bay, FL.

Haha...it's selfie time at the Eye Doctor's Office...while waiting to be called...haha... an hour and a half wait. Let's make use of our time while waiting...

Member KofC since 1994

*Frank had been a member of KofC quite & almost, quarter of century ago. Time really flies...
He is also a book author, A Touch of Life and The Thing of Beauty is a Joy Forever.*

My Spring Baby Upo.

LOOKING BACK...THERE ARE SO MUCH TO BE THANKFUL FOR

*L*ooking back... there are so much for me to be thankful for. As I tried to reflect on myself of what happened to my life after I left our Alma Mater in 1958 - it's hard for me to find words to best describe the gratitude I owed our school. Graduating from high school, had brought so much impact in my life. "What if?" is one of the questions that I asked myself, and who knows, maybe, some of you have the same question. For example: What if, I didn't go to high school or what if l didn't finish school? For me, attending high school was the greatest decision I ever made in my life. And I have no regrets about it. During that time, that was the best opportunity that knocked at my door.

Looking back...I remembered all the hardships, the sacrifices, and the struggles that we all made. We worked together, we studied together; we had some sorrows, we had some tears. Field work in the fishpond, field work in Panaguican and Libodan, field work in our respective field assignments, and field work after field work after strong typhoons hit our school. In spite of all those hard works and sacrifices, the 32 of us survived, of the remaining students of over 200 when we first began. Today, I salute you all for having made that commitment to go on...till the end. We were all heroes, the heroes of Class '58. Congratulations to us all for hitting the finish line as the first batch of graduates of the Agricultural and Fishery Curriculum. We're the beacon light for those left behind!

Looking back...I also owed so much to all our mentors. They nurtured us. They helped us opened our minds into the world of so many challenges and guided us to find answers to the mysteries of the unknowns. With all their best, and with all of their hearts, they tried to help made us a better person, a better person to our community, and to our country in general. Just to mention a few, I can never thank enough Mr. Aguilar, for opening my mind to the science of mathematics. I'm even embarrassed right now, to tell you that during my elementary years, math was my very least favorite subject. I was never impressed of my grades. I wanted also to thank the late Mr. Arcilla for helping me understand the science of physics, and to Mr. Pena the science of Chemistry. Without the help of these mentors, I could never be what I am today, a retired Engineer. Of course, I also owed my thanks to all my teachers, for making me a well-balanced person academically, with special mention to our late and beloved, Mr. Cabangon for opening my mind in the love of English and American Literature. When I went to college, I never had a back subject or behind in anything because my overall academic background was very well rounded. I excelled in most of my subjects. And I felt good about that in spite of the stress involved in maintaining a grade to retain my scholarship. Thank God for His grace and guidance during all those years.

Looking back...the greatest honor that I had ever known, was when I was awarded the honor, as valedictorian of class '58. Graduation day was the day, I learned that I was the valedictorian. That's when I was handed the graduation program. I cannot describe my joy during that moment. One thing they forgot, I wasn't asked to deliver my valedictory address. However, during the graduation pageant, I was the first participant to deliver my part. To me, that was a form of valedictory address... a farewell to my dear Alma Mater.

Looking back...my final thanks went to our beloved Alma Mater. Without that highest honor awarded to me, I could never be sure that I could pursue my college education because of my family meager means. Maybe I'll stay in Payo as a farmer or continue being a vaquero. With my transcripts of record as my passport to college, I was accepted at the Araneta University as a full time student on full scholarship. Plus, with a little bit of luck, my two elder sisters were able to help me in my other financial needs. I completed my college with honors. These helped me even better, to be accepted for graduate studies in Agricultural Engineering at the University of California. After this, I decided to stay in the USA. Considering all things, finishing high school was my stepping stone... to a much higher education and helped me realized my dream. God bless one and all.

By Francisco A. De La Rosa
CAIC Class '58 Valedictorian

Show your love!!

*To all Mothers in Heaven...HAPPY MOTHER'S DAY...
most specially to my beloved wife, MARY GRACE.*

Happiness is my PHOTOGRAPHY!

Upo is ready for harvest.

The KofC Gardeners @ Our Lady of Grace Catholic Church.

Frank On Canvas as a Professional Photographer, after graduation from The New York School of Professional Photography, New York, New York, 1983.

PANAGUICAN HILL

Still remember Panaguican Hill my old classmates dear?
In spite of our old age I hope you won't forget The four-year of fond memories
we had together At the foot of the beautiful Panaguican Hill.

The Panaguican Hill was our eyes and ears
When working in the fishpond with nothing but shorts
From morning till noon we worked so hard
And back to the classroom to open up our books.

The work in the fishpond was hard and back-breaking
The mud was heavy and the muscles were small
But the shadows of the tall and swaying coconut palms
Gave us shade to make us cool from the heat of the sun.

Down and up the hill we go
The higher we go up, the better the view
Applied to life, we learned a lesson
That the higher we achieved, the better we know.

I can never forget the incident that happened
While working in the fishpond alongside the foot of the hill Under the supervision of our instructor
who returned to the office And came back scratching his head, to see no students were around.

The students hid in the bushes of Panaguican Hill
Burst into laughter when the instructor had no more students in view However, with a little bit of
luck, our beloved principal forgave us Who understood what youthful indiscretion was all about.

Even though I live in a faraway land
I kept all my fond memories in my heart
All the hardships, the sacrifices and the struggles
At the foot of Panaguican Hill.

by Frank A. De La Rosa

Frank on canvas at his college graduation, @ the Araneta University, Philippines, '63.

With my daughter Cindy, the Pediatrician.

My beloved wife, Mary Grace, at home enjoying her flowers from the garden.

Frank & Mary Grace together anywhere, everywhere...

Republic of the Philippines
Province of Catanduanes
Municipality of Panganiban

OFFICE OF THE MUNICIPAL MAYOR MESSAGE

I am indeed inspired to greet every member of AAFS (CAlC) Class of '58 on your Golden Jubilee Reunion. Perhaps God will wonder that it's been years that you have assimilated what had been in the past is now an upbringing to the present. It is, however, worth mentioning and remembering yesterday's fond memories during your high school days with our Alma Mater, as it inspired and educated us to face the more difficult challenges in our lives. Without those memoirs we will not be what we are here today. Remember, it becomes a motivation for each other and everyone of CAlC Class '58 to pursue and reach everyone's goals in life. Let us not forget the lessons learned and the best memories that we had learned from our Alma Mater, but rather treasure and share them to the new generation.

As you celebrate your Golden Jubilee Reunion, I am confident that you will reminisce and travel back in time and recall the great days you stayed in our Alma Mater.

To you, Congratulations, and Mabuhay!

Sgd: Gregorio E, Angeles
     (Mayor)

In the Spring becomes a Rose. As sung by Bette Midler...... The Rose by Bette Midler Some say, "Love. It is a river That drowns the tender reed." Some say, "Love. It is a razor That leaves your soul to bleed." Some say, "Love. It is a hunger, An endless aching need." I say, "Love. It is a flower, And you its only seed."

A Gumamela flower in front of my house.

My beloved Mary Grace.

My beloved wife, Mary Grace loved to stroll down in our garden.

THE DISCOVERY OF MURPHY'S LAW

Murphy's Law, "If anything can go wrong, it will," was named after Capt. Edward A. Murphy, an engineer at Edwards Air Force Base, who in 1949 was working on Air Force Project MX981, a project designed to see how much sudden deceleration a person can stand in a crash. One day after finding that a transducer was wired wrong, he cursed the technician responsible and said, "If there is any way to do it wrong, he'll find it." The contractor's project manager kept a list of "laws" and added this one, which he called Murphy's Law. Actually, what he did was take an old law that had been around for years and gave it a name. Later, at a press conference, Dr. John Paul Stapp said that their good safety record on the project was due to a firm belief in Murphy's Law and in the necessity to try and circumvent it. Aerospace manufacturers picked it up and used it widely in their ads during the next few months and soon it was being quoted in many news and magazine articles. Murphy's Law was born.

Who was that skinny kid in the block? Barely tipping the balance @ 115 libras.

From the town of Panganiban... the Vaquero who visited Hollywood Universal Studios for the first time. He was hired right away. Look how strong he was even though he was so skinny. Haha...

Survivors of CAIC CLASS '58 GRADUATES. (CSU Panganiban Campus). Recent deaths: Miguel Cabañgon, Rosario Sumalde, Andres Ceballo and Benedicto Tugano, Jr....Our deepest condolences...from the members of Class '58.

@ the Broadway Musical. My Mary Grace was the Photographer.

Mr. Larry Hellman, Fire Chief
Fire Prevention Bureau
5240 Babcock Street NE Palm Bay, Florida 32905

Re: Brush Fires of March 2, 2007, Andrew St. SE, Palm Bay, FL

Dear Fire Rescuers of Palm Bay:

I found an opportune time to write you today. What a scary afternoon on March 2, 2007. Our neighborhood was on fire!

My wife and I were on our way to attend the Good Friday late afternoon Mass at Our Lady of Grace Catholic Church in Palm Bay. As we started to drive on Andrew Street, where we live, we saw a smoke at a distance. Suddenly we saw a fire starting at the end of Andrew St. Within seconds the fire became so big! We didn't have any chance to get anything valuable in the house. Strangers came to help us by spraying water on the roof, to the trees, and all over the lawn. Our neighbor across the street on Coconut Street said that they called 911. Thanks for their alertness. My wife and I, being in the state of shock, cannot do anything except to pray to the Heavens for God to help us stop the fire. Before our eyes, the miracles started to happen.

In a short time, the fire trucks came roaring on Andrew Street with brave and courageous men in it. You all now have total control of the raging fire. We asked God to give you strength and protection for your safety. How could we ever thank you for saving our house from fire? If we cannot thank you enough, God will in our behalf. Along with this letter is a picture that I took after the fire. Again, thank you all very much for the bravery you have shown. Congratulations! And God bless...

Very truly yours,
Frank & Mary Grace De La Rosa

I'm #1, first row, from the right.

Francis' confirmation...with Bishop Thomas Dorsey, Diocese of Orlando, FL, 1988.

Introducing: Our Bishop John G. Noonan, Diocese of Orlando, Florida.

My beautiful JFK Rose by the gate of my garden.

PERSONAL STORY
THERE IS NO DISTANCE IN PRAYER

It was over a year ago when I experienced the horror of watching a brush fire in our neighborhood. It was Good Friday, March 2, 2007, 1 could still remember. My wife and I were on our way to attend the Good Friday afternoon service. While I was backing out on our driveway, I saw a dark smoke at a distance not too far from us. I wasn't sure where it all started. I stopped for a moment. Suddenly, in few seconds, another fire started on the vacant lots next to our house. I believed that it was caused by the flying embers carried by the wind and landed on the dry brush underneath. That afternoon was very windy. The turn of the burning brush just happened so quick. I cannot believe my eyes. The towering inferno as high as the tall trees of mugho pines was coming too close to our house. It was real scary! I came to wonder whether there was any neighbor who was able to call 911. My wife and I were praying with open arms to the Heavens for our good and merciful God to stop the fire and to spare us our home, and all our neighbors. We didn't even have a chance to carry anything of value in the house. At this moment, we left everything in the hands of the God.

While we were praying, we heard the sound of the roaring fire trucks coming our way. At this time, many neighbors and strangers came to help us put up water on the roof, the plants, and the lawn. What a feeling of relief when you see people helping people. The firemen came at a very perfect time. Then with all their courage and strength, they aimed their giant nozzles to the raging fire. After a little while, I noticed that the fire had stopped just one yard before our fence. The wind changed its direction from going East to going North. As I looked around there wasn't any burnt houses, just the vegetation of cabbage palmettos, the tall mugho pines, the grass, and our neighbor's fence. How could we ever thank God for the miracle that happened before our eyes?

Yes, I believed that there is no distance in prayer. And above of all, I believed that there is no distance in God. God is as close as you believe Him to be. Keep praying... and believing. There is no greater power than the power of God. And to the power of prayers in our lives.

By Frank A. De La Rosa

Frank and Mary Grace lost in Paradise.

Frank in the garden of Eden.

Francis @ BS: in Civil Engineering graduation, 2000. University of Florida, Gainsville, Florida, USA. Magna Cum Laude.

Happy Celebration!

FOOD FOR THOUGHT

Contentment is not the fulfillment of what you want. It's the realization of how much you already have. When the door of happiness closes, another opens, but often times we looked so long at the closed door that we don't see the one which has been opened for us.

It's true that we don't know what we've got until we lose them, but it's also true that we don't know what we've been missing until it arrives. The happiest of people don't really have the best of everything, they just make the most of everything that comes along the way.

They say that it takes a minute to find a special friend; an hour to appreciate them; a day to love them; and an entire life to forget them.

The First Graduates of the Catanduanes Agricultural and Fishery School, Class '58.

Always Happy Together.

A Giant Florida Sunflower.

PEOPLE WHO KNOW HOW TO BRIGHTEN A DAY

People who know how to brighten a day
With heart-warming smiles
And with kind words they say,
People who know how to willingly share,
Who know how to give,
And who know how to care,
Who know to let all their warm feelings show...
Are people that others feel lucky to know.

-Amanda Bradley

Mom & Dad @ Francis' MS in Engineering Graduation at UF, Gainsville, FL. (with specialty in Transportation).

Green coconut back home.

My fragrant Pumeria/Calachuchi flowers in bloom. (Yellow-white variety).

MAY YOU ALWAYS HAVE AN ANGEL BY YOUR SIDE

May you always have an angel by your side
Watching out for you in all the things you do
Reminding you to keep believing in brighter days
Finding ways for your wishes and dreams
to take you to beautiful places
Giving you hope that it is certain as the sun
Giving you the strength of serenity as your guide
May you always have love and comfort and courage
Someone there to catch you if you fall
Encouraging your dreams
Inspiring your happiness
Holding your hand and helping you through it all
And may you always have
an angel by your side.

Attended a social function in Orlando, Florida.

With Fr. Wilmer Tria of Naga City Cathedral (Bicolandia).

DAY TO DAY LIFE VS. CHRISTIAN LIFE

Funny how a $ 10.00 bill looks so big when you take to church, but so small when you take it to the mall.

Funny how we get thrilled when a football game goes into overtime, but we complain when a sermon is longer than the regular time.

Funny how laborious it is to read a chapter in the Bible and how easy it is to read 200-300 pages of a best-selling novel.

Funny how people scramble to get a front seat at any game, but scramble to get a back seat at a church service.

Funny how we need 2 or 3 weeks to fit a church event into our schedule, but can adjust it for a social event at the last minute.

Funny how we can't think of anything when we pray, and don't have any difficulty thinking of things to talk about to a friend.

Funny how we are so quick to take directions from a total stranger when we are lost, but are hesitant to take God's direction to be found.

Funny how people are so consumed with what others think about them rather than what God think about them.

Funny how people think that they can get more accomplished in a lifetime without God than in an hour with Him.

Funny how people want to go to heaven, provided they don't have to believe, or to think, or to say, or to do anything.

Point to ponder: What you have to do or what you plan to is between you and God.

Kiss yesterday goodbye......

*We don't have to keep that Tux & gown.
Wear them! Make your evening special. Seize the moment.*

The Art in Photography by Frank De La Rosa.

My model sa Kamoteng Kahoy ng Kabukiran.

THINGS TO REMEMBER WHEN YOUR PARENTS GOT OLD:

*T*he day you find that I have become very old, try to have some patience with me, and try to understand me.

If I get dirty while eating...If I have some difficulty dressing...be patient! Remember the hours that I spent teaching you these things when you're small.

If I repeat the same thing dozen of times, do not interrupt me! Listen to me! When you were small, you kept asking me to read the same story, evening after evening, until you fall asleep. And I did it happily.

If I do not wash myself so often under the shower, do not reprimand and do not tell me that it is a shame.

Remember how many excuses I had to invent to walk you to a bath when you were small.

By seeing my ignorance of new technologies, do not laugh at me, but give me time to understand.

I taught you so many things...to eat well...to dress well...to behave well...how to confront the problems of life...

If sometimes I lose memory or am not able to follow a conversation, give me the necessary time to recollect and I do not become a nervous and arrogant person because the most important thing to me...is to be with you and to be able to speak to you.

If I refuse to eat, do not force me! I know very well when I am hungry and when I am not hungry.

When my poor legs will not allow me to move as before...Help me in the same way as when I held you your hands to teach you take your first step.

And when one day, I shall say I do not want to live anymore...that I want to die, do not get angry...because one day, you will also understand.

Try to understand that at certain age, we do not really live anymore. We simply survive!

One day you will understand that in spite of all errors, I always wanted what was best for you.

You do not have to feel sad, unfortunate or incompetent in front of my old age and of my state. You have to stay near me, try to understand what I live for.

Help me walk, help me to end my life with love and patience. The only thing that I need from you is smile and lot of love.

My two sons: Dex & Francis.

My daughter, Cindy, MD..at the De La Rosa - Nguyen Wedding.

Dancing with some old music of Bing Crosby......

$\mathcal{W}$arren Buffet, the second richest man in the world has something to say based on his personal life experience. Here they are:

1. Stay away from credit cards.

2. Money doesn't create a man; it is the man who created money.

3. Live your life as simple as you are.

4. Don't do what others say, just listen to them, but do what you feel good.

5. Don't go brand names; just wear those things in which you feel comfortable.

6. Don't waste your money on unnecessary things, just spend on those which you really are in need.

7. After all ifs your life, so why give chance to others to rule your life.

Tawag dito sa atin ay OLIVA. Dito sa US ay King Sago.

Looking back…"The Life of a Vaquero."

My Green Haven.

Welcome to the Walt Disney World, Orlando, FL.

SOULS...

The part of us that responds to beauty and goodness,
that inspires us to give of ourselves,
that calls us together to worship,
and draws us away for peaceful reflection.

The spirit is the tender place where hope flutters its
transparent wings, the gentle place where the candle
of faith steadfastly bums, the green place that
nurtures love, the dark place that harbors grief.

It is quiet place where we can be alone with our beliefs
in the Divine. And it is a place of compassion where
we can reach out to others in the practice of those beliefs.

Our spirits join us together even when we are strangers
and give us the words to speak to each other.

Our spirits lift us above the ordinary and open our eyes
to even the smallest wonders.

Spirit is the painter, the dancer, the teacher, the healer,
the lover, the dreamer that each of us carries within.

The KofC Honor Guard - 4th Degree - SK's.

During the installation of the Faithful Comptroller @ the Fr. Gabriel KofC Social Hall in Melbourne, Florida.

GOD KNOWS NO STRANGER

God knows no strangers, He loves us all
The poor, the rich, the great, the small.
He is a Friend who is always there
To share our troubles and lessen our care.
No one is a stranger in God's sight,
For God is love and in His light
May we, too, try in our small way
To make new friends from day to day.

...And... Suddenly, It's SPRING!

*My late beloved wife, Mary Grace's orchids are in bloom.
She took care of them and let them bloom for me.*

Let your imagination soars in your own backyard.

Another award from the KofC, #13234, OLOG.

INSPIRATIONAL QUOTATIONS:

"I looked on raising children not only a work of love and duty, but as a profession that demanded the best that I could bring to it."
 -Rose Kennedy

"Of all the rights of women, the greatest is to be a mother."
 -Lin Gutang

"Motherhood is the greatest privilege of life.
 -Roper Coker

"Every mother thinks her child is the most beautiful of all God's creations."
 -Yiddish Proverb

"Mothers shape the world as this shapes the lives of their children."
 -Mary Carlisle Beasly

"All that I am, or all that I hope to be, I owe to my angel Mother."
 -Abraham Lincoln

"Loving a child doesn't mean a giving into all his whims; to love him, to teach him to love what is difficult." -Nadia Binlanger

"Children are the hands by which we take hold of heaven."
 -Henry Ward Beecher

"A child is a beam of sunlight from Infinite and eternal."
 -Lymn Abbot

"Let every father and mother understand that when their child is three years old, they have done more than half of all they will ever do for character."
 -Horace Bushell

Pic-Art by Paco of Florida.

Special Portrait of my beloved wife, Mary Grace. By: Her loving husband, Paco.

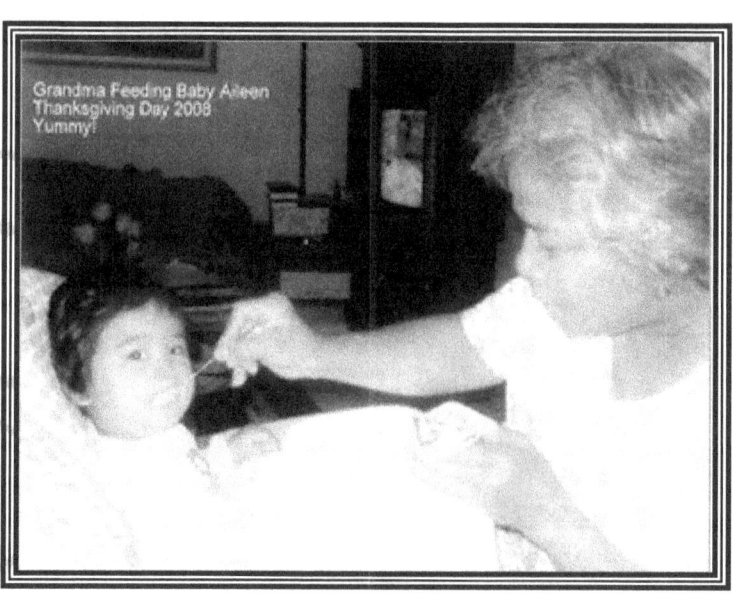

Priceless picture of Grandma with Baby Aileen.

Priceless picture of Quyen and her first daughter Aileen.

PERSISTENCE

"Nothing in the world can take the place of
Persistence.
Talent will not; nothing is more common than
unsuccessful men with talent.
Genius will not;
unrewarded genius is almost a proverb.
Education will not;
the world is full of educated failures.
Persistence and determination
alone are omnipotent."

-- Calvin Coolidge

My First Granddaughter & Me

A picture is worth more than a thousand words.

A visit to the Armenia Beach Resort in San Andres, Catanduanes, Philippines. Enjoyed eating & drinking the tender pulp and the fresh water from the green coconut...in 2008.

Ixora blooms in front of our Florida home.

My last pic. in the Phil. before leaving for America, the beautiful. '63.

LIVING LIFE ONE DAY AT A TIME

Our lives are made up of a million moments, spent in a million different ways. Some are spent searching for love, peace, harmony, and happiness. Others are spent surviving from day to day. But there is no greater moment than when we find that life - with all of its tears, sorrows, and joys - is meant to be lived and enjoyed one day at a time.

It's in this perspective in life that we find to discover the most wonderful and amazing truth there is… whether we live in a castle, surrounded by a couple of dozens of servants and wealth, or find it a struggle to live in a small nipa hut, we have within our power to be fully satisfied and live a life to the fullest meaning.

Living life one day at a time… we have that ability, by savoring each moment and rejoicing the day the Lord has given us. We can experience each day, with a fresh start, new hope, and aspiration, leading us make our dreams come true. Each day is new, and it enables us to truly enjoy life and live it to the fullest.

There may be times when we get up in the morning and things aren't the way we hoped they would be. There will be new challenges to face and changes that we have to experience in life and face it in our own special way. So when the days come to us that are filled with frustrations and disappointments, that's the time to remember that putting things in a more positive way, will bring forth positive results.

Talking about survivors. Survivors are people who have faced adversity and won. They've had all the odds against them, yet they've found a way to reach their goals and they don't allow themselves to live in pain forever. Like me I'm a survivor of three adversities as I journeyed through life in the past. Survivors face the future with purpose because they believe that God and time are on their side, and each effort will pay for itself. Survivors know how to make the best of life- by living life one day at a time.

As human beings, we're not perfect, and we're not supposed to be. But that's not always an easy thing for us to realize. The best thing we can do is to do the best we can, and always leave room for God to work on us. We don't make it alone in this world. We're lucky that there are people placed in our path to guide us, protect us, and touch our lives in their own special way so that we can get through it all… by living life one day at a time.

Our Lady of Grace Choir
Pastor: Fr. Emmanuel Akalue
Director of Music: James Sorrell
Photography by: Frank A. de la Rosa

Our Lady of Grace English Choir!

@ the Baptism of Aileen.

INSPIRATIONAL THOUGHTS TO PONDER:

Be thankful that you don't already have everything you desire.
If you did, what would there be to look forward to?
Be thankful when you don't know something,
For it gives you the opportunity to learn.

Be thankful for the difficult times.
During those times you grow.
Be thankful of your limitations,
Because they give you opportunities for improvement.
Be thankful for each new challenge,
Because it will build your strength and character.

Be thankful for your mistakes.
They will teach you valuable lessons.
Be thankful when you're tired and weary,
Because it means you've made an effort.

It's easy to be thankful for the good things.
A life of rich fulfillment comes to those
Who are also thankful for the setbacks.

Gratitude can turn a negative into a positive.
Find a way to be thankful for your troubles,
And they become your blessings.

My beloved wife, Mary Grace @ the Early Spring of 2009.

Frank, one of the Honor Guards, @ the Eugene Callagy's Funeral, St. Joseph Catholic Church, Palm Bay, FL.

It's gardening time in Florida!

One beautiful Spring day in Orlando, Florida. A view from the terrace of Hyatt Regency Resort, a place where luxurious weddings and parties are held.

THE VISITOR

*O*nce upon a time a very special Person came...and found the world unprepared. Just suppose, it happened again...and Jesus knocks at your door, what would you do?

If Jesus came to your house to spend a day or two,
If He came unexpectedly, I wonder what you'd do.
Oh, I know you would lodge Him as an honored Guest,
And all the food you served Him would be the very best;
And you would reassure Him you're glad to have Him there,
That serving Him in your house is joy beyond compare!
But when you saw Him coming, would you meet Him at the door
With arms outstretched in welcome to the blessed Visitor?
Or would you wish to tidy up before you let Him in?
Or hide some books to let the Bible lie where they had been?
Would you turn off the radio and hope He hadn't heard?
And wish you hadn't uttered that last, loud, hasty word?
Would you rush to hide your records and put some hymnal out?
Could you bid Jesus come right in- would you rush about?
I wonder if the Savior spent a day or two with you,
Would family conversation keep up to the usual pace?
And would find it hard each meal to say a table grace?
Would you sing songs you always sing and read the books you read?
And let Him know the things on which your mind and spirit feed?
Would you take Jesus with you each place you planned to go?
Or would you maybe change your plans for just a day or so?
Would you be glad to have Him meet your very closest friends?
Or would you hope they'd stay away until His visit ends?
Would you ask Him to have a walk in your garden and enjoy your flowers in bloom?
Or you would just give Him a basket full of fruits and vegetables for Him to take home?
Would you be glad if He would stay forever on and on!
Or you would you sigh with great relief when the Savior's gone?
It might be interesting to think of things that you would do-
If Jesus came in Person to spend some time with you.

Grandpa Frank with Luke & Sara @ home in Palm Bay.

My beautiful/Kayanga flower in my front yard.

My potted tropical Caimito fruit tree. I took care of it like a baby. During the cold spill in Florida, I moved my baby tree inside the porch. Warm & cozy corner.

My two potted Coffee plants inside the porch during the cold spill in Florida. I'll bring them outside as soon as it gets warmer.

INSPIRATIONAL THOUGHTS TO PONDER:

Do not undermine your worth by comparing yourself with others, it is because we are different that each of us is special.

Do not set your goals by what other people deem important. Only you know what is best for you.

Do not let your life slip through your fingers by living in the past nor for the future. By living your life one day at a time, you live all the days of your life.

Do not give up when you still have something to give. Nothing is really over until the moment you stop trying. It's a fragile thread that binds us to each other.

Do not be afraid to encounter risks. It is by taking chances that we learn how to be brave.

Do not shut love out of your life by saying it is impossible to find. The quickest way to receive love is to give love; the fastest way to lose love is to hold it too tightly.

Do not dismiss your dreams. To be without dreams is to be without hope; to be without hope is to be without purpose.

Do not run through life so fast that you forget not only where you have been, but also where you are going. Life is not a race, but a journey to be savored each step of the way.

The true color of FLORIDA!

How to create a work of art with a lampshade!

@ the San Francisco Fisherman's Wharf. At the background, shows the Panoramic view of the SF Golden Gate Bridge.

Good bye Shuttle DISCOVERY.

DON'T WE ALL?

I was parking in front of the mall wiping my car one summer afternoon. I had just come from the car wash and waiting for my wife after shopping at the mall. Coming my way from across the parking lot was what society would consider a bum. From the looks of him, he had no car, no home, no clean clothes, and no money. There are times when you feel generous, but there are times that you just don't wan to be bothered. This is one of those "don't want to be bothered times." "I hope he doesn't ask me for any money," I thought. He didn't. He came and sat on the curb in front of the bus stop. After a few minutes he spoke, "That's a pretty car," he said. He was ragged but he had an air of dignity around him. His scraggly brown beard keeps more than his face warm. I said, "Thanks," and continue wiping off my car. He sat their quietly as I worked. The expected plea for money never came.

As the silence between us widened something inside said, "Ask him if he needs any help." I was sure that he would say "yes" but I held true to the inner voice. "Do you need any help?" I asked. He answered in three simple words that I shall never forget.

Sometimes in our life, we take simple things for granted. Oftentimes we look for wisdom in great men and women. We expect it from those of higher learning and accomplishments. This time I expected nothing but an outstretched grimy hand. Instead, he spoke these three words that shook me. "Don't we all?" he said.

I was feeling high and mighty, successful and important, above a bum in the street, until those three words changed my life forever. "Don't we all?" needed help. Maybe not for a bus fare or a place to sleep. I needed help but different from that man or anybody else. I reached in my wallet and gave him not only enough for bus fare, but enough to get a warm meal and shelter for the day.

Those three little words still ring true. No matter how much you have, no matter how much you have accomplished, you needed help too. No matter how little you have, no matter how loaded you are with problems, even without money or a place to sleep, you can still help. Even it's just a compliment like the man said, "You have a pretty car." Or just a simple smile, you can give that. Remember that a good deed no matter how small is never wasted. A simple word of praise is easy to speak, and the echo it makes is endless.

You never know when you may see someone that appears to have it all. They're waiting for you to give them what they don't have. A different perspective, a glimpse at something beautiful, a respite from a daily chaos, that only through torn word can see. Maybe the man was just a homeless stranger wandering the streets. Maybe he was more than that. Maybe he was sent by a power that is great and wise, to minister to a soul too comfortable in themselves. Maybe God looked down, called an Angel dressed like a bum, then said, "Go minister to that man cleaning the car, that man needs help." DON'T WE All?

Ripe Atis up on a tree in my tropical garden.

KNIGHTS HELPING KNIGHT

It was the 20th of December 2009 at 3:00PM when Our Lady of Grace became the host for the 6th day of Novena of "Simbang Gabi (Filipino Mass)' also called Mesa de Gallo during the olden times, in conjunction with the Filipino Ministry, Diocese of Orlando. I was chosen then to be the Coordinator from Our Lady of Grace, to organize the Mass Entourage and the Program for the reception after the Mass. I was just given three weeks to coordinate for all the Filipinos, and the Filipino Americans in the whole Brevard County. It was indeed a job, but it paid for itself at the end.

I needed around 20 people to assist in the Mass. I could get most of them from the Filipino group, but the others like the assisting Deacon, Sacristan, Altar Server, and the Eucharistic Ministers, I have no other choice than to ask help from our church and the Knights of Columbus.

I'm most thankful to the members of the Knights of Columbus for helping me in behalf of Our Lady of Grace to fill in the assistance I needed for the Mass. Thanks to Fr. Leo Hodges for concelebrating the Mass with Fr. Peter Cordeno from Holy Cross Catholic Church in Orlando, to Deacon Kevin Crawford for assisting Fr. Peter, to the Sacristan, Bill McSween, and to the two Eucharistic Ministers namely: Brother Knights Willie Jenkins and Gary Nolte. All the names I mentioned are members of the Knights of Columbus, Council #13243, except of course Fr. Peter.

My wholehearted thanks to you, Brother Knights for helping me in my time of need. Your assistance and kindness are very much appreciated. Peace and God bless..

By Frank A. De La Rosa, 4th Degree

Yellow on Blue.

A sonnet by Elizabeth Barrett Browning.

So sad....Four friends in this picture had returned to their Creator.

A multicolored Squash.

THE GIFT OF FAITH

No greater gift has God given us than the gift of faith; that deep and steadfast inner knowing that no matter what happens, we can call upon the help of higher power, higher than ourselves, to see us through.

Were it not for our faith, we would not dare to dream the dreams we reach and strive for. Were it not for our faith, we would give up too soon, back down too quickly, and walk away too abruptly from the challenges and obstacles that appear in our paths. Were it not for our faith, we would abandon those who need us when times get tough. Were it not for our faith, we would turn our backs on our own neighbors when disaster or tragedy strikes.

Faith is the invisible glue that binds us together, that holds us fast to our visions of what our lives can be. Without faith, we are weak, frightened creatures hiding our heads in the sand. Without faith, we would have never become the free and powerful people that we are. Just remember how the American people responded to the wake of 911. It's because of faith. Without faith, we would have never dared to try anything that's impossible to do, or tried to survive in moment of tragedy.

But with faith we can do anything, be anything. We can climb the highest mountain and touch the stars. We can fall and get up and fall and get up again, never surrendering, never giving in. With faith, we are warriors of the heart and spirit, bold and brave and true. Let's give thanks to our good God for giving us the Gift of Faith.

My Nanay & Tatay,

Autumn is the air in Florida! The beautiful bloom of my Golden Tree told me so.

A Portrait of my Hybrid Hibiscus by Frank A. de la Rosa.

Some gentle thoughts to ponder:

Like a flame in darkness night; kindness fills the heart with light; pass the torch of kindness on; love will light in the dawn.

No act of kindness, however small, is ever wasted.

The most wasted day is that in which we have not helped.

Let the joy in your heart overflow and water everyone you meet.

People will forget what you did; people will forget what you said, but people will never forget how you made them feel.

If you light a lamp for somebody, it will also brighten your path.

When the mind thinks of success, the outside world mirrors these thoughts. The image you have of yourself is responsible for the way people see and treat you.

A happy mind manifests success.

My Golden Rain Tree is in bloom for the Fall season.

CA...Testimonial Survivor...from a grandfather of 8: It's Thanksgiving Lord, and during this very especial occasion, I cannot let it go without foremostly thanking you for giving me another new life to live, and another chance to do things for your greater glory. Right now Lord, you could see it. Thanks for guiding me & inspiring me having this gr

Located at the overhung structure in front of my house.

TO: MS. NOVETT P. MCKENZIE
(Belated Letter of Thanks)

*W*e had always thought of writing you. Tomorrow comes...tomorrow goes...and that tomorrow becomes today. Today, we found and have your address. So, there's no more excuse for not writing you today. Therefore thank God with humble heart for giving us today.

Yes, indeed... at times we get so caught up in our own lives that we unknowingly forgot to respond our hearts to those nice people around us who in their own simple ways did ordinary things in an extraordinary way, by touching lives of other people in their own special way. Looking back...what's today without your help?

With this thought in mind, it is important that you receive the recognition and appreciation which you greatly deserved. Putting this on paper will help us get this message to you and the echoes it makes will make you a very special person for all those who knew you and the community at large.

We know you will never stop caring or making a difference - to touch other people's lives. What you did to us during those most difficult times in our lives will be treasured in our hearts forever. Again, thanks so much for everything. God bless..

With our warmest regards,
Frank & Mary Grace

My Sweet Potato Patch. Good for talbos for sinigang na Bangus.

My Gabe (elephant ears), Tanglad (Lemon grass) and Sweet Potato (Camote) Corner.

Photo courtesy by: Gloria Abad Suan

Aerial View of Our Lady of Grace Catholic Church. Photo by: Paco of Florida.

LET'S BE A TEAM

Let's put the past behind us and move ahead,
Making things happen, working together instead.
Keeping in mind that we all made mistakes,
Tripping over ourselves, looking for breaks.

Let us start today, as if life were new,
Judging people only on what we hear them say and do.
No one is perfect, everyone makes mistakes,
There are more good people than there are fakes.

Judge each person as an individual, keeping in mind,
Someone exactly like you, you will never find.
If you could, you won't want it that way,
For you would be bored with them in less than a day.

Accept people with their faults, for you have some too.
Don't try to change them, don 't let them change you.
You can only be you, and I only me.
Let's spend our time together the best we can be.

If we can do this and join as a team together,
We can make many things happen,
no matter how stormy the weather.
In the end what a team can accomplish,
Is everyone's dream, everyone's wish.
LET'S THEN BE A TEAM!

Frank's Bar,

The Philippine Shell.

Advent Season's Greetings!

PORTRAIT OF FRIENDSHIP

I can't give solutions to all life's problems, doubts or fears.
But I can listen to you, and together we can seek answers.

I can't change your past with all its heartache and pain, nor the future with its untold stories. But I can be there with my thoughts and prayers.

I can't keep your feet from stumbling, I can only offer my hand that you may grasp it and not fall. Your joys, triumphs, successes, and happiness are not mine. Yet I can share in your laughter and joy. Your decisions in life are not mine to make, nor to judge. I can only support you, encourage you, and help you when you ask.

I can't give you boundaries which I have determined for you. But I can give you the room to change, room to grow, room to be yourself.

I can't keep your heart from breaking and hurting. But I can cry with you, pick up the pieces and put them back in place.

I can't tell you who you are. I can only share with your joys, sorrows with all of its tears, and be your friend.

My granddaughter is an altar server at St. John Vianney Catholic Church.

From Orlando with

"Portrait by Selfie"

A self-portrait.

THANK YOU LORD

Thank you Lord for this child
You have given to us
To love and care for and everyone
To bring up faithfully.

Thank you Lord for his smile
That brightens up our days
Thank for his joy and laughter
We see when he plays.

Thank you for his beautiful eyes
That watch all that we do
His little hands and little feet
That want to follow too.

Thank you Lord for each day
With this child that you give to us
May he learn Your love and ways
on us and now we live.

Baby Jesus is the reason for the season!

My grandchildren joined us at the celebration of life of their Lolo Peter, last Sunday, Dec. 16th.

JUST FOR LAUGHS

This is a story about two New Yorkers, best friends, who decided that they had had it with city living, so they decided to purchase a ranch in Texas in order to live off the land like their ancestors.

The first thing they have to do - to have their plan works was to have a mule to pull the plow. So they went to a neighboring rancher and asked him if he had any mule to sell. The rancher said, "No sorry."

They were disappointed but continued talking with the rancher for a few minutes more. One of them spotted a bunch of honeydew melons stack against the barn and asked, "What are those things?"

The rancher, seeing that they were city slickers, decided to have some fun. "Oh/' he answered, "Those are mule eggs. You take one of those eggs home and wait for it to hatch and you will have your mule."

The city slickers were overjoyed, so they bought one of the melons, placed it in the back of their pickup, and drove down the bumpy road toward their own spread. Suddenly they hit an especially bad bump and the honeydew melon bounced out of the back of their pickup, hit the road, and busted open. Looking into his rearview mirror the driver saw what had happened and slammed on the brakes, turned the truck around and dove back to retrieve their mule egg.

Meanwhile a big old Texas jackrabbit came hopping by and saw the honeydew burst open in the road. He hopped over to it and standing in the middle of the mess began to eat it. At about that time the two city slickers friends came running toward the smashed melon and spied this long-eared Texan creature in the middle of it! One of the friends shouted, "Our mule egg has hatched! Let's get our mule!

Herbal: My Pandan plant in my yard. I used it for cooking rice & suman and other Filipino cooking.

Ito ang inyong lingkod...Mang Frank. Theme song: Moonlight Serenade by Glenn Miller.

The Breath of Spring!

*Spending an evening by the laughing water.
A loving memory with my beloved wife, Mary Grace.*

THE BEAUTIFUL ACT OF GIVING

*G*ive to those less fortunate than you are...With an open heart.
Give smile to everyone you meet... Smile with your eyes.
Give a kind word...With a kindly thought behind the word.
Give appreciation... With a warmth from the heart.
Give time for a worthy cause...With eagerness.
Give hope...The magic ingredient for success.
Give happiness...A most treasured state of mind.
Give encouragement...The incentive to action.
Give cheer...The verbal sunshine.
Give pleasant response...The neutralizer of irritants.
Give good thoughts...Nature's character builder.
Give prayer...The instrument of miracles.
The list is endless...

EVEN WITHOUT WORDLY WEALTH OR MATERIAL POSSESSIONS, IT'S POSSIBLE FOR EACH OF US TO BE GENEROUS. WITHIN EACH OF US ARE SO MANY ANSWERS AND POSSIBILITIES.

THERE'S SO MUCH THAT WE GIVE, IF WE REALLY TRY, IN OUR ROUTINE EVERYDAY LIVING. SO MUCH INNER JOY TO BE FOUND EACH DAY IN THE "BEAUTIFUL ACT OF GIVING."

Dear God,

*W*e thank you for the earth; for the wide sky of blue and the blessed sun, for the ocean and streams, for the towering hills and the whispering wind, for the trees and green grass.

We thank you for our senses by which we hear the songs of birds, and see the splendor of field of golden wheat, and taste autumn's fruit, rejoice in the feel of snow, and smell the breath of spring flowers.

Grant us a heart wide to all this beauty, and save us from being so blind that we pass unseeing, even the common thorn bush is aflame with your glory.

For each new dawn is filled with infinite possibilities for new beginnings and new discoveries. Life is constantly changing and renewing itself. In this new day of new beginnings with God, all things are possible. We're restored and renewed in a joyous awakening to the wonder that our lives are and, yet, can be. Amen.

Lolo Frank & Baby Anderson - my youngest grandson.

THE ROSE WITHIN

A certain man planted a rose and watered it faithfully and before it blossomed, he examined it. He saw the bud that would soon blossom, but noticed thorns upon the stem and he thought, "How can any beautiful flower come from a plant burdened with so many sharp thorns?" Saddened by the thought, he neglected to water the rose, and just before it was ready to bloom .. .it died.

So it is with many people. Within every soul there is a rose. The God-like qualities planted in us at birth, grow amid the thorns of our faults. Many of us look at ourselves and only see the thorns, the defects. We despair, thinking that nothing good can possibly comes from us. We neglect to water the good within us, and eventually it dies. We never realize our potential.

Some people do not see the rose within themselves; someone else must show it to them. One of the greatest gifts a person can possess is to be able to reach past the thorns of another, and find the rose within them. This is one of the greatest characteristics of love...to look at a person, know the true faults and accepting that person into your life...all the while recognizing the nobility in the soul. Help others to realize they can overcome their faults. If we show them the "rose" within themselves, they will conquer their thorns. Only then they will blossom many times over. Happy Valentine's Day To All!

A Priceless Work of Art (Father & Son).

PHOTOGRAPHY

*P*hotography is more than just
A gift to bring or send.
And more than just a likeness of
A relative or friend.

It is a kindly greeting and
A memory to hold.
Of happy times and pleasant things.
However new or old.

It is a mirror that reflects
Companionship and cheer.
And now and then the wistfulness
That turns into a tear.

A photograph is something to
Adorn a desk or a wall.
Or carry in a pocket and
Display to one and all.

It is a faithful portrait
The smile that friendship shares
To add the sunshine and to show
That someone really cares.

LIVE A LIFE THAT MATTERS

Whether you are ready or not, someday your life will come to an end.

There will be no more sunrises, no minutes, hours, or days.

All the things you collected, whether treasured or forgotten, will pass to someone else.

Your wealth, fame, and temporal power will shrivel to irrelevance.

It will not matter what you owned or what you were owed.

Your grudges, resentments, frustrations, and jealousies will finally disappear.

So, too, your hopes, ambitions, plans and to-do list will expire.

The wins and losses that once seemed so important will fade away.

It won't matter where you came from, or on what of the tracks you lived at the end.

It won't matter whether you were beautiful or brilliant, even your gender and skin color will be irrelevant.

So what will matter? How will the value of your days be measured?

What will matter is not your success, but your significance.

What will matter is not what you learned, but what you taught.

What will matter is every act of integrity, compassion, courage or sacrifice that enriched, empowered or encouraged others to emulate your example.

What will matter is not your
 competence, but your character.

What matter is not how many people
 you know,how many will feel a lasting loss when you are gone.

What matter is not your
 memories,but the memories that
 live in those who love you.

What will matter is how long you will
 be remembered,by whom and for what.

Living a life that matters doesn't
 happen by accident. It's not a matter
 of circumstances,but of choice.
 Choose to live a life that matters.

-Anonymous

50th year in America celebration.

FOOD FOR THOUGHT

*Y*ou must give some time to your fellowmen. Even it it's a little thing, do something for others - something for which you get no pay but the privilege of doing it.
-Albert Schweitzer

We make a living with what we get, we make a life by what we give.
-Winston Churchill

And as we let our own light shine, we unconsciously give other people permission to do the same.
As we are liberated from our own fear, our presence automatically liberates others.
-Nelson Mandela

REFLEcnONS

OX TAIL KARE-KARE

*I*ngredients:

4 or 6 pieces of ox tail, cleaned & fats removed
1 big bundle of yard long beans or string beans, cut into 2 inches long
1 banana heart, sliced finely crosswise or dried oriental lilies
1 big onion. Sliced
3 cloves garlic, crushed
4 Oriental eggplant, cut into one inch lengths
3 small radishes, peeled and sliced
1 1/3 Cup toasted rice, powdered
1 Cup toasted peanuts, ground or peanut butter
2 tablespoons of food coloring, achuete

Procedure:

Clean the cut-up ox tail and remove fats as much as you can. If the pieces are too big, please ask the butcher at the super market to cut them up for you into small pieces, like half or so. Boil the ox tail a night before until tender before you finally cook it, to allow the fats to solidify. The following day, remove all the solidified fats floating on the surface of the kettle or sauce pan. Saute the garlic and onion, and then add the cooked ox tail. Pour the mixture in the sauce pan and the water in which the ox tail was cooked. Add salt to taste. Boil. Add the sliced banana heart or dried oriental lilies and cook until tender. Then add the string beans, eggplants, and radish. Wash the seeds of the achuete (for food coloring) and soak in one half cup of water. Add this colored to the mixture. Then add the powdered rice, and peanut butter, stirring thoroughly to avoid sticking. Serve with Bagoong or shrimp paste sauted in garlic. Enjoy!

OUR DEEPEST FEAR...

Our deepest fear is not that we are inadequate.
Our deepest fear is that we are powerful beyond measure.
It is our light, not our darkness, that most frightens us.
We ask ourselves, who am I to be brilliant, gorgeous, talented and fabulous?
Actually, who are you not to be?
You are a child of God.
Your playing small doesn't serve the world.
There is nothing enlightened about shrinking so other people
won't feel insecure around you.
We were born to make manifest the glory of God that is within us.
It's not just in some of us,
it's in everyone.

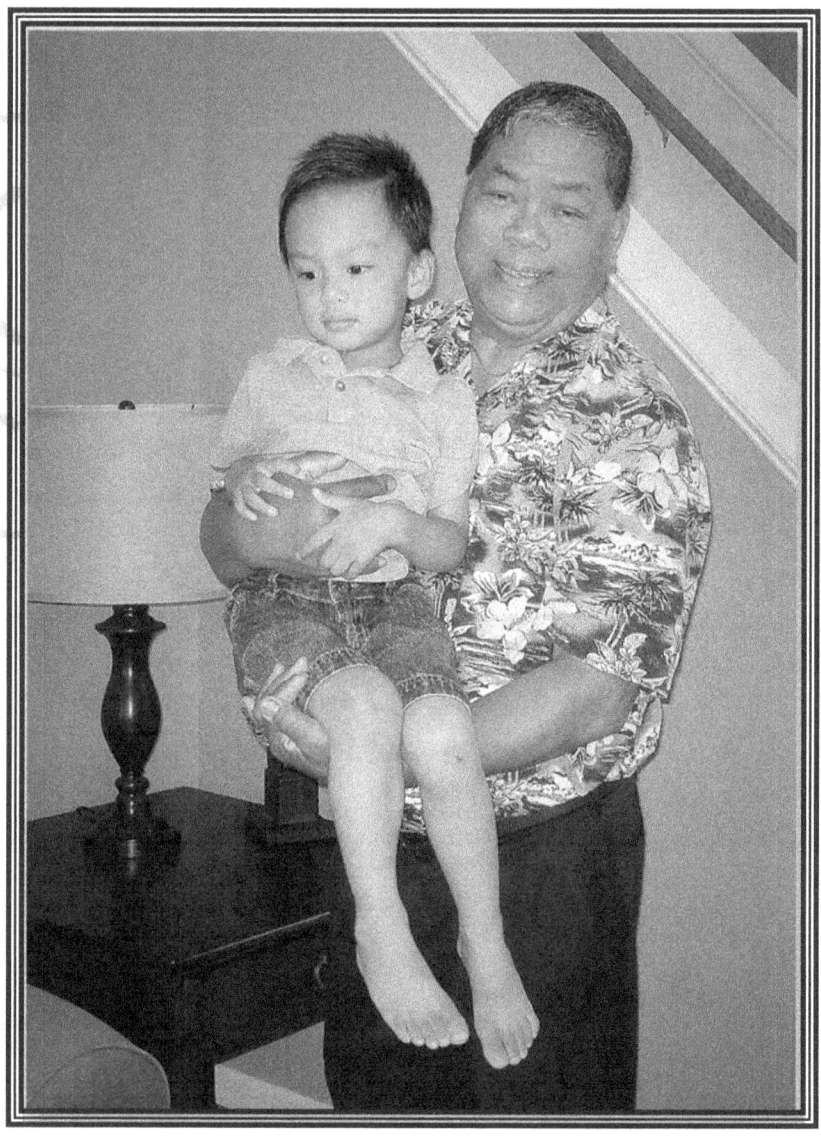

Lolo Frank with his grandson, Nico, Tampa Florida.

DEAR LORD

Dear Lord, teach us your patience and your forgiveness. Show us how to be more tolerant of others, more accepting of their differences, for it is these differences that make our nation so unique. We put our trust in you, dear Lord, that you will keep watch over us as a loving father keeps watch over his children. Amen.

9/6/2019

LIVE UP TO YOUR DREAMS!

*D*on't underestimate your worth by comparing yourself with others. It is because we are different; each of us is special. Don't set your goals by what other people deem important. Only you know what is best for you. Don't take for granted the things closest to your heart. Cling to them as you would your life, for without them, life is meaningless. Don't let your life slip through your fingers by living in the past or for the future. By living your life one day at a time, you will live all the days of your life. Don't give up when you still have something to give. Nothing is really over until the moment you stop trying.

Don't be afraid to encounter risks. It is by taking chances that we learn how to be brave. The quickest way to receive love is to give love; the fastest way to lose love is to hold it too tightly, and the best way to keep love is to give it wings. Don't give up your dreams; to be without dreams is to be without hope; to be without hope is to be without purpose. Don't run through life too fast that you forget not only where you've been, but also where you are going. Life is not a race, but a journey to be savored each and every step of the way. Life is beautiful, enjoy it! Life is a song, sing it! Life is a dream, dream it. And above all, life is a gift from God, a gift so precious in His sight. We can never thank Him enough for this!

Our First Caribbean Cruise, 2005.

9/6/2019

LETTER FROM HEAVEN

To my dearest family, some things I'd like to say. But first of all, to let you know, that I arrived okay.

I'm writing this letter from heaven and I dwell with God above.

Here, there's no more tears of sadness; but just eternal peace, happiness and love.

Please do not be unhappy just because I am out of sight. Remember that I am with you every morning, noon and night. That day I had to leave you when my life on earth was through. God picked me up and hugged me and He said, "I welcome you;

It's good to have you back again, you were missed while you were gone. As for your dearest family, they will be here later on.

I need you here badly, you're a part of my plan.

There's so much that we have to do, to help our mortal man."

God gave me the list of things, that He wished for me to do. And the foremost on the list, was to watch and care for you. And when you lie in bed at night the day's chores put to flight. God and I are closest to you...in the middle of the night.

When you think of my life on earth, and all those loving years. Because you are only human, they are bound to bring you tears. But do not be afraid to cry: it does relieve the pain.

Remember there would be no flowers, unless there was some rain.

I wish that I could tell you all that God has planned. If I were to tell you, you wouldn't understand.

But one thing is for certain, though my life on earth is over. I'm closer to you now, than I ever was before.

There are many rocky roads ahead of you and many hills to climb; But together we can do it by taking one day at a time.

It was always in my mind and I'd like it for you too;

That as you give unto the world, the world will give to you.

If you can help somebody who is in sorrow and pain; Then you can say to God at night...

"My day was not in vain."

And now I am contented...that my life was worthwhile. Knowing as I passed along the way I made somebody smile.

So if you meet somebody who is sad and feeling low; Just lend a hand to pick him up, as on your way you go.

When you're walking down the street and you've got me on your mind;

I'm walking in your footsteps only half a step behind.

And when it's time for you to go... from your body to be free. Remember you're not going... you're coming here to me.

ONE SOLITARY MAN

He was born in an obscure village, the child of a peasant woman. He grew up in another village, where he worked in a carpenter shop until he was thirty. Then for three years he was an itinerant preacher. He never wrote a book. He never had an office. He never had a family or owned a home. He didn't go to college. He never visited a big city. He never traveled two hundred miles from the place he was born. He did none of the things that usually accompany greatness.

He had no credential but Himself. He was only thirty three when the tide of public opinion turned against Him. His friends run away. One of them denied him. He was turned over to His enemies and went through the mockery of a trial. He was nailed to the cross between two thieves. While he was dying His executioners gambled for His garments, the only property he had on earth. When He was dead, He was laid in a borrowed grave through the pity of a friend. Twenty centuries have come and gone, and today He is the central figure of the human race.

All the enemies that ever marched, all the navies that ever sailed, all the parliaments that ever sat, all the kings that ever reigned, put together, have not affected the life of man on this earth as that "One Solitary Life".

A memory of my life at the Nursing School.

OBLATIONS (FROM "DO IT ANYWAY" -VERSION BY MOTHER TERESA OF CALCUTTA)

People are often unreasonable, irrational, and self-centered.
Forgive them anyway.

If you are kind, people may accuse you of selfish, ulterior motives.
Be kind anyway.

If you are successful, you will win some unfaithful friends and some genuine enemies.
Succeed anyway.

If you are honest and sincere people may deceive you.
Be honest and sincere anyway.

What you spend years creating, others could destroy overnight.
Create anyway.

If you find serenity and happiness, some may be jealous.
Be happy anyway.

The good you do today, will often be forgotten.
Do good anyway.

Give the best you have, and it will never be enough.
Give your best anyway.

In the final analysis, it is between you and God.
It was never between you and them anyway.

I HAVE NEVER MOVED A MOUNTAIN

Lord, I've never moved a mountain
And I guess I never will,
All the faith that I could muster
Wouldn't move a small ant hill.

Yet, I'll tell You, Lord, I'm grateful
For the privilege knowing Thee,
And for all the mountain-moving
Down through life You have done for me.

And when I needed grace to lift me
From depths of deep despair,
And when burdens, pain and sorrow
Have more than I could bear

You have always been my Helper
To restore life's troubled sea,
And to move these little mountains
That have looked so big to me.

Many times when I've problems
And to God I have to pray,
And the worries and the heart aches
Just kept mounting everyday.

Lord, I don't know how you did it
Can't explain the where's or why's,
All i know I have seen these mountains
Turn to blessings in disguise.

No, I've never moved mountains
For my faith is far too small,
Yet I thank You, Lord, of Heaven
You have always heard my call.

As long as there are mountains
In my life I have no fear,
For the mountain-moving Jesus
He shall make them disappear.

Dad & Francis, Wildwood Beach, Summer 1985.

THE SERENITY PRAYER

*God, grant me the Serenity
to accept the things I cannot change.
The courage to change the things I can,
and the wisdom to know the difference.*

*Living one day at a time, enjoying one moment at a time;
Accepting hardship as a pathway to peace;
Taking, as Jesus did, this sinful world as it is;
Not as I would have it;*

*Trusting that You will make all things right
if I surrender to Your will;
So that I may be reasonably happy in this life
and supremely happy with You forever in the next.*

AMEN

-Reinhold Niebuhr

THE AMERICAN NATIONAL ANTHEM
(The Stars-Spangled Banner)

O! say can you see, by the dawn's early light,
What so proudly we hailed at the twilight's last gleaming,
Whose broad stripes and bright stars through the perilous fight,
O'er the ramparts we watched, were so gallantly streaming?
And the rockets' red glare, the bombs bursting in air,
Gave proof through the night that our flag was still there;
O! say does that star-spangled banner yet wave
O'er the land of the free and the home of the brave?